A Child's History of Britain

Life in Anglo-Saxon Britain

Anita Ganeri

Raintree is an imprint of Capstone Global Library Limited, a company incorporated in England and Wales having its registered office at 7 Pilgrim Street, London, EC4V 6LB – Registered company number: 6695582

www.raintreepublishers.co.uk
myorders@raintreepublishers.co.uk

Text © Capstone Global Library Limited 2014
First published in hardback in 2014
The moral rights of the proprietor have been asserted.

Edited by Nick Hunter and Penny West
Designed by Joanna Malivoire
Original illustration © Capstone Global Library Ltd 2014
Illustrated by: Laszlo Veres (pp.26-7), Beehive Illustration
Picture research by Mica Brancic
Originated by Capstone Global Library Ltd
Production by Helen McCreath
Printed and bound in China

ISBN 978 1 406 27049 5
18 17 16 15 14
10 9 8 7 6 5 4 3 2 1

British Library Cataloguing in Publication Data
A full catalogue record for this book is available from the British Library.

Acknowledgements
We would like to thank the following for permission to reproduce photographs: © The Trustees of the British Museum p. 7; akg-images pp. 18 (North Wind Pictures), 20 (British Library); Alamy pp. 6 (© Eyre), 8 (© geogphotosfilm), 9 (© Mark Boulton), 10 (© geogpix), 17 (© Ivy Close Images), 22 (© geogphotos), 23 (© Krys Bailey), 27 bottom right (© Eyre), 27 top left (© Eyre); Getty Images pp. 5 top (The British Library/Robana), 11 (The British Library/Robana), 12 (The Bridgeman Art Library), 14 (The British Library/Robana), 15 (Gallo Images/Danita Delimont), 19 (Hulton Archive), 21 (Christopher Furlong), 24 (National Geographic/ Ted Spiegel); The Bridgeman Art Library p. 16 (The Stapleton Collection/Private Collection); The Picturedesk pp. 5 bottom (The Art Archive/ Jarrold Publishing), 25 (The Art Archive/Ashmolean Museum); West Stow Anglo-Saxon Village p. 13.

Cover photograph of Alfred presenting a royal cloak and sword to his grandson Athelstan reproduced with permission of Harry Mileham (Private Collection/The Bridgeman Art Library).

We would like to thank Heather Montgomery for her invaluable help in the preparation of this book.

Every effort has been made to contact copyright holders of material reproduced in this book. Any omissions will be rectified in subsequent printings if notice is given to the publishers.

Disclaimer

Contents

Anglo-Saxon Britain 4

Who was in charge? 6

Where would I live? 8

What would my childhood be like? 10

What clothes would I wear? 12

What would I eat and drink? 14

How would I have fun? 16

What would I believe? 18

What would I do when I grew up? 20

How could I become a warrior? 22

After the Anglo-Saxons 24

How do we know? 26

Map 28

Quiz 29

Glossary 30

Find out more 31

Index 32

Some words are shown in bold, **like this**. You can find out what they mean by looking in the glossary.

Anglo-Saxon Britain

From around **AD** 400, warriors from Europe began to invade Britain. They sailed across the North Sea, looking for new lands to settle in. They are now known as the Anglo-Saxons.

Before the Anglo-Saxons arrived, southern Britain was part of the Roman **Empire**. The Roman army left Britain in AD 410, leaving the way open for new settlers. The Anglo-Saxons were a mixture of people from lands that are now Germany, Denmark, and the Netherlands. Gradually, they took over most of England, dividing it into seven kingdoms. They pushed the **Celtic** Britons into Wales, Scotland, and Cornwall.

TIME OF INVASION

Around AD 400	Anglo-Saxons begin to settle in Britain
AD 597	St Augustine brings Christianity to Britain
Around AD 600	Seven Anglo-Saxon kingdoms created
AD 793	First recorded attack by Viking raiders
AD 886	Alfred the Great becomes King of Wessex
1042	Edward the Confessor becomes king of all England
1066	Battle of Hastings; Norman forces conquer England

HISTORY BOOK

In the 9th century, King Alfred ordered **monks** to write a history book about the Anglo-Saxons. It was called the Anglo-Saxon **Chronicle**. It gives a year-by-year account of battles, harvests, diseases, **famines**, and unusual events, such as **eclipses**.

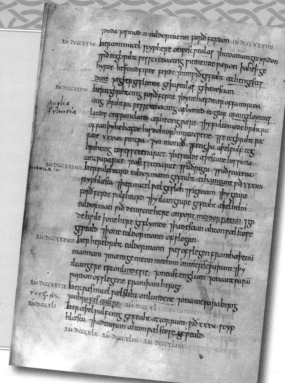

Pevensey Castle in Sussex was built by the Romans to keep the Anglo-Saxons out.

Who was in charge?

At first, the Anglo-Saxons lived in small family groups. Gradually, these groups grew larger and were ruled by war-chiefs or kings. By **AD** 800, the seven largest kingdoms in England were Northumbria, Mercia, East Anglia, Wessex, Essex, Sussex, and Kent. The kings regularly went to war with each other to try to take more control.

This is a model scene showing how an Anglo-Saxon king was buried.

Thanes and churls

The king was the most powerful person in Anglo-Saxon times. Next came the **thanes** (nobles) who helped the king to rule. Most ordinary people were **churls**. These free people fought for the thanes and worked on their lands. Beneath them were slaves who were mostly prisoners of war. If your family were slaves, you belonged to a master and had no freedom or belongings of your own.

Offa was King of Mercia from AD 757 to 796. He is famous for building a huge earth wall along the border with Wales and for making England's first silver pennies.

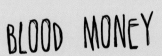

BLOOD MONEY

Everyone in Anglo-Saxon society was worth a certain amount of money, depending on his or her **rank**. This was called **wergild**. If a person was killed, the killer had to pay the correct amount of wergild to the victim's family.

Where would I live?

If you had been a child in Anglo-Saxon Britain, you probably would have lived in a small village, with several other families. You shared your home with your parents, grandparents, and other relations. Most houses were built of wood and had **thatched** roofs.

If your parents were **churls**, your house was small with one room for living and sleeping in. In the middle was a fireplace. A big metal cooking pot hung from a chain over the fire. The fire also heated and lit your home. There were no chimneys and only slits for windows, so the house got very smoky inside. You sat and slept on wooden benches.

Inside an Anglo-Saxon house, you can see the fire and cooking pot in the middle of the room.

window slit

cooking pot

wooden bench

fireplace

An Anglo-Saxon house had a simple shape and was built of wood with a thatched roof.

If your father was a **thane,** you lived in a larger hall in the middle of the village. Your father owned the fields and land all around. The floor of the hall was covered in **rushes**. Sometimes, animals were kept at one end.

What would my childhood be like?

Anglo-Saxon girls learnt to weave wool to make cloth on a **loom** like this one.

There were no schools in Anglo-Saxon times, and most children could not read or write. If you were a girl, your mother taught you the skills you needed to look after a house. For example, you learnt to cook, brew ale, and weave cloth. Fathers taught their boys different skills. Boys learnt to hunt, fish, fight with weapons, and plough a field. The sons of kings or rich **thanes** sometimes had tutors (private teachers) at home.

Growing up

In Anglo-Saxon times, people married at a young age. Girls were usually around 12 years old and boys around 14. You were allowed to choose whom you wanted to marry, but it was important that your parents approved. People usually married someone of the same **rank** as themselves. If you were a **churl**, you married a churl. If you were a slave, you married a slave.

Anglo-Saxon boys helped with farming jobs, such as haymaking.

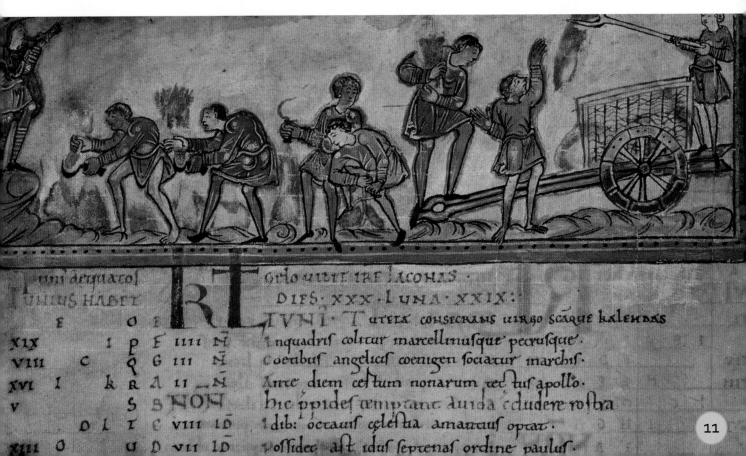

What clothes would I wear?

Anglo-Saxon men and boys wore knee-length **tunics** with belts. In cold weather, they wore long cloaks and trousers wrapped around their legs with thin, leather strips. Women and girls wore long dresses with belts, and long cloaks. They often covered their heads with a scarf. Both men and women used metal pins or brooches to fasten their cloaks.

This is an Anglo-Saxon brooch, made of gold with silver, garnets, and pieces of shell.

Poor people's clothes were made from rough wool from sheep and goats. If you were a girl, you learnt to spin the wool and weave it into thread on a **loom**. You helped your mother to make clothes for your family. Rich people wore clothes made from finer wool or **linen**, and decorated with embroidery and even silk.

ANGLO-SAXON AMULETS

The Anglo-Saxons believed in magic, and many wore lucky charms around their necks. These were called **amulets**. People believed that they kept their wearers safe in battle and protected them from illness and evil spirits.

This woman is dressed in Anglo-Saxon-style clothes.

What would I eat and drink?

Your everyday meals would mostly be made up of foods that your family grew. You ate bread made from wheat or rye, oat porridge, and stew made from carrots, leeks, onions, beans, and peas. You also had milk and cheese from the village cows and sheep, and eggs from the hens. Sometimes, you ate fish that you caught in the sea or river. Meat was for special occasions.

This man is looking after pigs until they are ready to eat.

Feasting

The **thane** sometimes held a great feast for the villagers in his hall. People sat on benches around a long table. A pig was roasted, or a wild boar if the thane had been out hunting. This was eaten with bread. The food was cooked over a fire in the middle of the hall. There was plenty of ale and mead to drink.

THIRSTY WORK

River water was often dirty, so everyone, including children, drank beer made from barley. Very rich people also drank wine, and mead, a strong beer made sweet with honey.

Rich people drank from drinking horns or glass goblets, called claw beakers.

How would I have fun?

People worked hard in Anglo-Saxon times, but they also liked to enjoy themselves. Holidays were a good chance for villagers to get together and have fun. They took part in outdoor sports, such as wrestling, weightlifting, tug-o-war, and ball games.

Children also enjoyed board games, using dice and counters, and "knucklebones", where you had to toss five small bones or stones into the air and catch them in different ways. You also played with homemade toys, such as wooden animals, rag dolls, and spinning tops.

Here, children are playing blind man's bluff (also known as blind man's buff).

Stories and songs

The Anglo-Saxons liked listening to poems and stories about brave warriors. The most famous was about a warrior called Beowulf. He killed monsters and dragons and became king of his people. Often, the stories were set to music and sung at feasts.

Beowulf fights a fearsome dragon with a mighty sword.

RIDDLES

The Anglo-Saxons loved telling riddles. These are guessing games with words. One riddle said: "I cover the ground like a blanket, and melt in the midday sun". Can you guess the answer?

Answer: snow

What would I believe?

At first, the Anglo-Saxons worshipped many gods and goddesses. They believed that the gods ruled over the world and controlled what happened in people's everyday lives. Some of our days of the week get their names from Anglo-Saxon gods. Wednesday is named after Woden, the king of the gods. Friday is named after Frige, the goddess of love.

Odin, king of the gods in Viking beliefs, became the Anglo-Saxon god, Woden.

In AD 597, the **Pope,** the leader of the Christian Church in Rome, sent a **monk** to England. The monk was called Augustine, and his job was to **convert** the Anglo-Saxons to Christianity. Augustine arrived in Kent, where he persuaded King Ethelbert to become a Christian. King Ethelbert allowed Augustine to build a church in Canterbury. Over the next hundred years, many other Anglo-Saxons also became Christians.

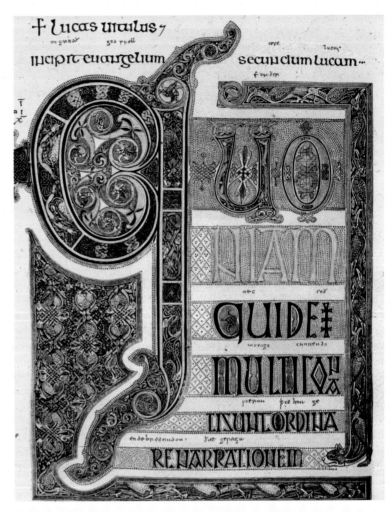

This is a page from the Lindisfarne Gospels, dating back to the 7th century AD.

MONASTERIES

Some Christians became monks. They built **monasteries** in which they lived, prayed, and studied. Monks made beautiful, handwritten books, such as the Lindisfarne Gospels, which were decorated with pictures and patterns. A monk called Bede lived in the monastery at Jarrow in Northumbria. He wrote a famous book about the Anglo-Saxons and how they became Christians.

What would I do when I grew up?

In a village, most people worked as farmers. They grew crops and kept animals, such as sheep, pigs, and cows. Men worked together to plough the fields, with heavy wooden ploughs pulled by oxen. You might be sent ahead to sow seeds and scare away the birds. If you were older, you also herded cows and sheep with your dog.

This illustration is from about 1030 and shows farmers ploughing a field.

Craftspeople

Some villagers had special skills. Potters made clay pots for eating and cooking, and for holding the ashes of the dead. Leather workers made shoes, belts, bags, and buckets. Woodworkers made benches, chests, bowls, and carts. Metalworkers made brooches and beautiful gold and silver jewellery for rich people.

Here is a small part of the Staffordshire hoard.

TREASURE CHEST

In 2009, thousands of gold and silver Anglo-Saxon objects were found in a field in Staffordshire. Sword handles and decorations showed off the amazing skills of the metalworkers.

Some Anglo-Saxons worked as traders. They sailed to Europe in small wooden boats, taking wool and slaves to sell. Back in England, some trading centres grew into towns. By the mid-7th century AD, the Anglo-Saxons were also making their own coins.

How could I become a warrior?

Most Anglo-Saxons were part-time warriors. You went into battle if your **thane** or king ordered you to. After battle, you went back to your farm to look after your crops and animals. Training for battle began at an early age. You started practising fighting with wooden weapons when you were around eight years old. Sports, such as running, jumping, and wrestling, were also good training for war.

These people have dressed up as Anglo-Saxon part-time warriors.

Into battle

In battle, Anglo-Saxons fought on foot. They carried spears, axes, swords, knives, and wooden shields. Swords were very precious and were often handed down from fathers to their sons. Most warriors did not have metal armour but wore thick leather waistcoats. To protect themselves from enemy weapons, they formed a "shield wall". They stood side by side, holding their shields in line.

WARRIOR CODE

Anglo-Saxon warriors followed a strict "warrior code". This taught that a warrior must be brave, strong, and loyal to his thane or king. He must be ready to fight to the death for his leader. At the same time, he had to be humble and kind.

Here, King Alfred is armed with his sword and shield.

After the Anglo-Saxons

This carved stone shows Viking warriors attacking Lindisfarne.

At the end of the AD 700s, the Vikings began to attack England. The first place they raided was Lindisfarne in Northumbria. They destroyed the **monastery**, killed many of the **monks**, and stole their treasure. Later, they attacked the east and south coasts, and raided Ireland.

In the AD 870s, the Vikings attacked the Anglo-Saxon kingdom of Wessex. King Alfred drove them back, but he later made peace with them. The two sides agreed to divide England between them. Alfred ruled the south and west. The Vikings ruled the north and east, known as the Danelaw.

Alfred's son, Edward, and grandson, Athelstan, won control of the Danelaw. However, under later kings, the Vikings won back their lands. In 1016, a Viking called Canute became king of England. He died in 1035, and his sons ruled after him. Finally, in 1042, Edward the Confessor became king and England had an Anglo-Saxon ruler again.

This beautiful jewel was made during King Alfred's reign. It was the handle of a stick used to point at the words while reading the Bible.

END OF THE ANGLO-SAXONS

When Edward died in 1066, Harold, Earl of Wessex, became king. But a few months later, William the Conqueror invaded from France. At the Battle of Hastings, Harold was killed and William became king, ending the Anglo-Saxon period.

How do we know?

In May 1939, **archaeologists** in Sutton Hoo, Suffolk, made a remarkable discovery. As they dug the earth from an ancient burial mound, they began to uncover the outline of an enormous ship. They had found a ship grave, the traditional way of burying an Anglo-Saxon king. In the centre of the ship lay a burial chamber. It was filled with treasure, including jewellery, weapons, armour, cups and spoons, and fragments of clothes.

This is a copy of a helmet from the Sutton Hoo ship burial. It is covered with pictures of brave warriors fighting.

This is a copy of a gold purse lid from the Sutton Hoo ship burial. It covered a leather pouch for gold coins.

Map

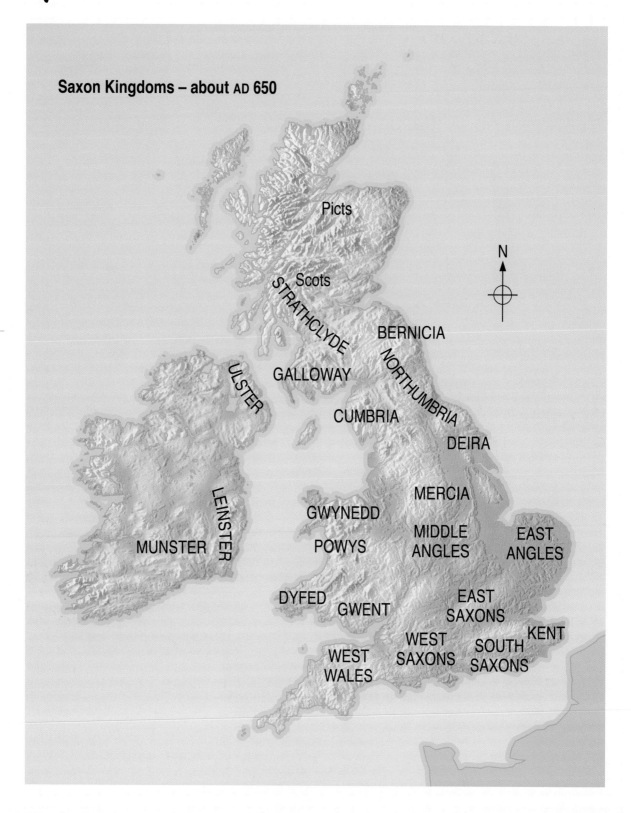

Saxon Kingdoms – about AD 650

Picts

Scots

STRATHCLYDE

BERNICIA

ULSTER

GALLOWAY

NORTHUMBRIA

CUMBRIA

DEIRA

LEINSTER

MERCIA

GWYNEDD

MIDDLE ANGLES

EAST ANGLES

MUNSTER

POWYS

DYFED

GWENT

EAST SAXONS

WEST WALES

WEST SAXONS

SOUTH SAXONS

KENT

N

Quiz

What do you know about life in Anglo Saxon times? Try this quiz to find out!

1. What were Anglo-Saxon nobles called?
   a churls
   b thanes
   c slaves

2. What language did the Anglo-Saxons speak?
   a Old Norse
   b Old German
   c Old English

3. How was wergild calculated?
   a on your rank in society
   b on your height and weight
   c on your bravery in battle

4. How did Anglo-Saxon men keep their trousers up?
   a with belts
   b with strips of leather
   c with zips

5. What did most people drink?
   a water
   b fruit juice
   c beer

Answers
1. b
2. c
3. a
4. b
5. c

Glossary

AD dates after the birth of Christ; these count upwards, so AD 20 is earlier than AD 25

amulet lucky charm worn around the neck

archaeologist person who finds and studies places and objects from the past

Celts people who lived in Britain before the Romans arrived

chronicle record of events in the order in which they happened

churl ordinary Anglo-Saxon who was a free man or woman

convert persuade someone to join a new religion

eclipse when one heavenly body, such as the Sun or Moon, is blocked by another

empire group of states and territories under the rule of one country

famine time of very little food

linen cloth made from the flax plant

loom machine for turning wool into cloth

monastery community of monks

monk man who lives in a monastery and dedicates his life to God

Pope head of the Roman Catholic Church, which is based in Rome, Italy

rank place or position in society

rush grass-like plant with long leaves and stems

thane Anglo-Saxon nobleman who owned a large hall

thatch roof made from straw

tunic long, sleeveless, dress-like shirt

wergild amount of money based on a person's rank in society

Find out more

Books

Anglo-Saxons and Vikings, Abigail Wheatley and Hazel Maskell
    (Usborne, 2012)

Beowulf (Young Readers), Rob Lloyd Jones (Usborne, 2009)

Men, Women and Children in Anglo-Saxon Times, Jane Bingham
    (Wayland, 2010)

The Anglo-Saxons in Britain (Tracking Down), Moira Butterfield
    (Franklin Watts, 2013)

Websites

www.bbc.co.uk/schools/primaryhistory/anglo_saxons
See the BBC website for facts, activities, pictures, and videos about life in Anglo-Saxon times.

www.britishmuseum.org/explore/young_explorers/childrens_online_tours/anglo-saxon_england/anglo-saxon_england.aspx
Look at Anglo-Saxon objects in the British Museum.

www.show.me.uk/topicpage/Anglo-Saxons.html
Have a look at this website for information and fun activities, including taking part in a virtual dig at an Anglo-Saxon village.

www.suttonhoo.org
The Sutton Hoo Society works with the National Trust to look after the site.

Places to visit

There are Anglo-Saxon sites to visit in many parts of Britain. You can find out about them through the following organizations:

English Heritage
www.english-heritage.org.uk

The National Trust in England, Wales, and Northern Ireland
www.nationaltrust.org.uk

The National Trust of Scotland
www.nts.org.uk

Index

Alfred, King 4, 5, 23, 25
amulets 13
Anglo-Saxon Chronicle 5
archaeologists 9, 26
armour 23, 26, 27
Augustine, St 4, 19

battles 13, 22, 23
beakers 15
Bede 19
beer and wine 15
beliefs 13, 18–19
Beowulf 17
burials 6, 26–27

Celtic Britons 4
children 10–11, 12
Christianity 4, 19
churls 7, 8, 11
clothes 12–13, 26
coins 7, 21
craftspeople 20, 21

Danelaw 25

Edward the Confessor 4, 25
entertainment 16–17
Ethelbert, King 19

families 8
farming 20, 22

feasts 15
food and drink 14–15
furniture 8

games and toys 16
gods and goddesses 18

halls 9, 15
Harold, King 25
Hastings, Battle of 4, 25
houses 8–9

invasions 4, 25

jewellery 12, 20, 25, 26

kingdoms 4, 6, 28
kings 6, 7, 22, 23, 26

language 11
Lindisfarne 24
Lindisfarne Gospels 19

magic 13
marriage 11
monasteries 19, 24
monks 5, 19, 24

Normans 4, 25

Offa, King 7
Old English language 11

Pevensey Castle 5
poems and stories 17

ranks 7, 11
riddles 17
Roman Empire 4

ship graves 26–27
skills 10, 20, 21
slaves 7, 11, 21
society 6–7
sports 16, 22
Staffordshire hoard 21
Sutton Hoo 26–27

thanes 7, 9, 10, 15, 22, 23
trade 21
tutors 10

Vikings 4, 24–25
villages 8–9

warrior-code 23
warriors 22–23, 24
weapons 22, 23, 26
weaving 10, 12
wergild 7
West Stow 9
William the Conqueror 25
work 20–21